to the light

a collection *of* songs & stories

by Anne Heaton

Published by Spill It Publishing
PO Box 11901
Shorewood, WI

©2019 Anne Heaton
anneheaton.com

First Edition Printing, Printed in the USA
ISBN 978-1-698-26087-7

Artwork by Barbara Heaton: barbara-heaton.squarespace.com/about-avenue
Cover design by Liz Kalloch, Anne Heaton and Barbara Heaton.

For my daughters Rosemary Cecilia and Helen

preface

Pema Chodron refers to a Hopi Prophecy which says we no longer live in the time of the lone wolf. Instead, it advises that we look and see who is around us. To me this means that it's more important than ever to create and live collaboratively. Each of these songs was sparked by some personal interaction or global event that touched my life. In this way, these songs were born out of collaborations with life itself and with the people who appear in them. As I recorded my album, I wanted to continue in this collaborative spirit and stay connected to my music community across the country. As each song was written, I thought of a musician-friend who might help me bring it fully to life. Then I reached out to that person.

Last year, I hosted an online series called "How the Song Came to Be" where I interviewed songwriters about their writing tools, creative practices and the stories behind their songs. I've always loved stories and the interesting and magical ways songs are written. Sometimes it's like walking around in the dark feeling for the next wall. Other times, the work unfolds over a longer period of time, involving the intersection of multiple events. For me, there are always lessons in creating; sometimes I need to surrender to the work, ask for help, cultivate courage, or practice patience. Maybe I need to put myself in new situations or simply wait to live the experiences that will tell me which way to go next. Songwriting, and creating of any kind, is a spiritual practice for me, as is uncovering the lessons it imparts. It's my intention that in sharing these songs and stories, others will also share their stories with me, with themselves, and with each other.

That the collaboration goes on, that is my deepest wish.

Feel free to grab a pen, your favorite journal and cup of tea or coffee while you listen and read as there are reflection questions at the end of each song chapter.

–Anne

foreword

In this collection Anne invites us into these stories and songs and in the process, she encourages us to share our own experiences. She says, "When we hear the stories of others, we experience the creation of a bridge." This book is a bridge. It prompts us into asking the deeper questions in our own lives, and into caring for our own stories with such tenderness. These songs are as generous as Anne's spirit. They reach out to us, they inspire us to connect and to create.

For many of us, it has felt as though the darkness has loomed larger in recent years. What we need most in a dark time are artists who help us reframe, who help us see "the essential goodness" and who keep us turning toward the light and toward one another, even when our hearts are gripped with fear.

These songs are luminous with gratitude and celebration. A gratitude that grows out of a deep understanding of loss. I've had the entire range of experience as I listen. The deep belly laughs of "The Donut Song". The goosebumps on a clear autumn day as I listened to "Hannah". I remember crying with happiness when I first heard a recording of "Joy". I was standing on a busy street corner in downtown Boston. I remember the moment my fear and grief lifted. That softening, that moment of turning my face toward the morning sunlight.

These songs and stories have been such good spiritual companions to me. I know they will be good friends to you also.

Step on into the circle. Bask in the light.

from Meg Hutchinson

Artists spend a lot of time alone, thinking about, building, creating, editing, re-editing and birthing their work. By the time they are ready to share the work, it is usually at least somewhat polished and/or in a "finished" state. Every once in a while, we're let into a creation part-way through and it feels like the most amazing gift: getting to jump on an artist's superhighway of inspiration as a passenger and come along for the ride.

With these stories, directives and thoughtful questions, Anne is not only letting us in to her process as an artist, she is offering a template to find our true selves. The book you are holding is like the most intimate episode of "Behind The Music" only you get to be an audience of one. It feels as if Anne is speaking directly to you, the reader, because she is! She not only *wants* to share the what, how and why of this amazing collection of songs, she has to!

As true masters come to know, once they know the truth, they have only one choice: to give it away. This book is going to become your favorite guide, the one you keep dog eared and by your desk, in your bag at all times, or beside your altar or workspace because it isn't just a workbook. It is also the portrait of a masterful story-teller, a gracious and humble student and a wise and compassionate teacher. This collection isn't about witnessing a private process, it's an invitation to a roundtable discussion on beauty, deep listening, sorrow and its transformation. So take a seat, dig in and return to this book again and again as it guides you to all the magic that's already yours.

from Natalia Zukerman

contents

 joy

In January 2017, my neighbor Susie suggested I write a song for the DC Women's March, "a sing-a-long for the bus". I said no, I didn't think I could do it, but the idea wouldn't let me go.

I grieved that prior year while watching the news, worrying about the kind of world my 5 and 7-year old daughters would grow up in. Like many others, I didn't want my mood, energy level and contributions to be influenced by ongoing negative narratives. I wanted to remember what connects all of us in a time where media told us we were irrevocably divided.

I reflected on my truth outside of a state of reaction. What's important to me? How do I connect to my deepest self and values? How does the way I start my day affect everything else?

At the last minute, I was invited to play a small concert near the march, hosted by Natalia and Arianna Zukerman and including artists such as Mona Tavakoli, Chaska Potter, Edie Carey, Becky

Gephardt, Sara Bush and Sara Bareilles. This inspired me to finish the song in time to play it for these women.

I turned and looked squarely at my fears, feeling how tender and vulnerable it felt to be raising girls at this time. I also reflected on my love of nature and the quiet of morning. I considered the people who were making a positive impact, like Amma who gives hugs worldwide, Bill Gates and his invitation to innovate to zero emissions, and Pope Francis' call to extend mercy. A woman whose email list I happened to be on, Carol CC Miller, who frequently organized free hugs days even wove her way into the song.

> I reflected on my truth outside of a state of reaction. What's important to me? How do I connect to my deepest self and values? How does the way I start my day affect everything else?

"Joy" was born out of my desire to reconnect with what I love, to be rooted in the essential goodness and calm that's always there for us though sometimes it's deep below the waves.

Joy

I've got nothing against you
I just want to be heard
Like every child, woman and man
In this big beautiful world
I knew boys like you in high school
Thought if I ignored, you'd go away
But what I fear grows, what I resist persists
I need joy to be my best

How do I look on you with joy in my heart?
Look on you with joy in my heart?

I get up before the sunrise
Look at the stars in the night sky
I breathe in and out slowly
I let my fears rise up out of me like smoke floating over the sea
I find the joy in my heart early
Open my eyes to the birds, the trees

I feel joy in my heart
Joy in my heart

Joy in the world, joy in the world, joy in the world

I read the Hiding Place, Lived through an arms race
Knew at 4, I'd not retaliate
Against the bomb, if up to me

'Cause then there'd be no place to be
Oh no not a gun in every school

Digging in the ocean for dirty fuel
Backing out of what we agreed to
And I fear the worst

With joy in my heart
Joy in my heart

The way you look at something changes things
The way you look at something changes things

So who're you gonna be? How're you gonna see?
Some say it's mercy
Others give hugs for free
Some try to get us to zero
I see kids in New York from every land
Who don't know any different
Laughing and holding hands
While parents watch them play

With joy in their hearts
Joy in their hearts

Joy in the world, joy in the world, joy in the world

Reflection Questions ··

What brings you joy?

When, if ever, has a painful experience brought about a transformation or change in circumstances that led to more joy in your life?

In what ways do you experience joy outside of your circumstances?

In what ways do you experience joy because of your circumstances?

Is it possible to generate joy? If so, how?

Creativity Key: Intimacy

To write this song, I had to get cozy with my greatest fears, with what fills up my heart and with what helps me transcend my daily circumstances. By peeling back the layers of the generalized anxiety I felt, I found vulnerability, hope and a desire to invite others to do the same.

[celebration song

On a cold February morning, a few weeks after moving to Ann Arbor, as I forced myself to unwrap and put away utensils and books, my 4-year old daughter sauntered through the living room, put her hands in the air and did an impromptu hip shake while singing, "I feel a celebration going on." I thought to myself, "You do?" I was accustomed to her singing made-up melodies from her car seat, narrating the things we'd pass along the road: "There's a tree, growing like me" or "Birdy, birdy flying." But on this day, I was particularly struck with how in touch she was with happiness on a grey day, in a new town without her cousins or toys. I wondered if I too could "feel a celebration going on" even while unpacking boxes on a bleak winter morning.

I took it as a challenge to see if I could access my inner celebration. I thought if I made a list of all the things that made me happy, I'd be able to write it, but it didn't quite work.

Then, one morning, I argued with my husband over coffee. He offered to reheat mine. I cringed because a fresh pot is so much yummier. So we made a fresh pot which we enjoyed together.

> This simple exchange triggered memories of all the situations in my life where I learned that every moment, no matter how challenging, is leading to this current, perfect, present moment.

This simple exchange triggered memories of all the situations in my life where I learned that every moment, no matter how challenging, is leading to this current, perfect, present moment. My painful divorce led to a better relationship and two children. A car accident helped me feel my spirit more. Thich Nhat Hanh, who trained as a monk during the Vietnam War, cultivating peace in wartime, said, "a lotus grows in the mud." I loved and clung to those words.

Having this theme helped the song tumble out. I even felt moved to bring the idea to climate change, which is so overwhelming, it can be hard to see the miracles of nature that are right in front of us.

Celebration Song

I don't reheat my coffee
I put a brand new pot on
When I drop my child at preschool
I might have a sparkly dress on
If I want to drive, if I want to fly
Who's gonna stop me?
No one but me, and what if I don't?

I feel a celebration going on

I feel the bottoms of my feet
Walking to a pulse on the street
On our warming globe
Trees rise to absorb the storm
They reach up to the sky
Pine and Oak for you and I
Green waving at the blue
Breathing in the CO2, thank you!

I feel a celebration going on

When I think how lost I felt en route to this perfect moment
All that had to go right and wrong for me to come here and own it
How unlikely we'd meet, make up after fights
That I'd take the 59th Street Bridge to you one night

How you and I rolled a Crown Vic on black ice, I was hit by a
drunk driver, but somehow survived, though I flew across the free-
way, I didn't have a scratch, my spirit shifted up above my head

and it was cause of that that later I knew, when I walked through

hard times, I had a spirit to turn to. Can you feel it, can you feel it,

rising up?

How my grandpa showed me the ballads out of Ireland
My friend Motley the music of Harlem
How I always preferred though I didn't know it then the music of
the oppressed over those oppressing them
How my mom got me all those piano lessons. Damn. Thank you.
Can you feel it, can you feel it, rising up?

So I could make my music, share it in my own voice
How I had to meet the wrong man to make a better choice.
How it all had to burn down so I could rebuild my life and have
these two daughters who like ice cream and watermelon best
They like red wagon rides and their new blue dresses.
They feel it, rising up

And maybe humanity won't survive but I'm gonna make the most
of my time. Like Paul McCartney said: maybe you've been waiting
your whole life for this moment to arise. Like Thich Nhat Hanh
lived peace in Vietnam, he kept rebuilding and rebuilding. He
helped Martin Luther King over here as they kept marching and
marching

Can you feel it? Can you feel it? Can you feel it?

Can you feel a celebration going on? (A celebration, a celebration)
Can you feel a celebration going on? (A celebration, a celebration)

Reflection Questions ⋯⋯⋯⋯⋯⋯⋯⋯⋯⋯⋯⋯⋯⋯⋯⋯⋯⋯⋯

How do you like to celebrate?

Do you celebrate big and small things?

What was one of your favorite celebrations ever?

What's something you haven't celebrated yet that you still would like to?

Do you prefer to celebrate others? If so, why?

Creativity Key: Connection

At first, I wanted to call this Creativity Key "Honesty" because when we're in touch with the truth about ourselves, it's easier to reach out to others and connect in meaningful ways. What do I mean? Well, when we know and share what makes us tick, what makes us laugh, what hurts and what we desire, others feel let into our world. They begin to imagine similar experiences they've had or if they haven't had them, they're inspired to try and relate. Likewise, when we hear the stories of others, we experience the creation of a bridge. Stories are bridges. What are some bridges you've built? What are some bridges others have built to you?

hannah

When I first met her in Bogotá in 2008, Hannah talked to me using whirling hand signals, widening her eyes and making loud animated sounds. She was so excited to tell me her story. Hannah had a mental disability and her family had forced her to do intense manual labor in the Colombian jungle, transporting huge barrels of water and other loads through the hills.

One day, several men who worked in the oil business were flying overhead in a helicopter and saw something shiny and moving. It was Hannah's water barrel. They went down to see what it was, and they met Hannah. One of the men was Jaime Jaramillo who later founded an organization that rescues neglected children from the streets and sewer systems of Bogotá and Manizales.

After talking with Hannah's family and realizing they were not willing to care for her, they took Hannah to Bogotá, enrolled her in school and she now lives at one of the centers for rescued children. It is a loving environment surrounded by friends and teachers where she enjoys stickers, Hannah Montana, and dancing.

Hannah was born different
Grown she cannot speak
Her parents don't see the blessing
So they work her on hills so steep

Hannah

Hannah Hannah on the ground
Calls the helicopter down
It's caught their eye
A shiny thing
What is that she's carrying?

The workers fly down
There she is
Crawling along a jungle path
Small and friendly Hannah
With a barrel strapped to her back

What am I doing here
Carrying this heavy load?
The whirring from above is so exciting
What a surprise to be rescued by a bird

Hannah was born different
Grown she cannot speak
Her parents don't see the blessing
So they work her on hills so steep

Even though she is in pain
Hannah's got a smile
Brighter than the lights of Bogota
And she gives it to the men from the sky

What am I doing here
Carrying this heavy load?
The whirring from above is so inviting
What a surprise to be rescued by a giant bird
Coming down from the sky
What a surprise
I'm ready to fly away

She's happy here in Bogota
No more bruises on her back
But Hannah still sees people
On their concrete jungle paths

A banker with his cigarette
Drivers crawling by
She sees it in their faces
When they look up at the sky
Wondering....

What am I doing here
Carrying this heavy load?
Whirring from above would be so exciting
What a surprise to be rescued by a giant bird
Coming down from the sky
What a surprise
I'm ready to fly away

Reflection Questions ···

Have you met a person who inspired you to be more loving or appreciative? If so, who?

Have you ever heard a story that is so unbelievable it seems like a miracle? How did it make you feel? Do you believe in miracles? What is a miracle to you?

Have you met someone who "on paper" is worse off than you but seems to have discovered some secret to happiness? Who was this person and what were the circumstances?

Creativity Key: Inspiration

I was so inspired by this joyful person who'd endured so much that I felt I simply must share her story.

rise

In 2012, I went on a songwriting retreat – it's a long story – hosted on the Weezer Cruise. Yes, that means the band Weezer was there, playing live every night. I was grouped with two other songwriters, Beth Wood and Shannon McNally, and we were asked to write and record two songs in three days.

We holed up in a tiny room with a little round boat window and talked about our lives, relationships and being on the road. We also talked about Ghost Dancing and the beautiful land of America. We wondered aloud what compelled us to travel this country playing the songs we wrote to small groups of people, often to our financial detriment.

It reminded me of the Hopi Prophecy. As touring singer-songwriters, we could relate to that feeling of being a lone wolf. But here we were, together in a room, with the chance to look around, see and create something new with the people around us.

When we got stuck, I went to Weezer shows because there's nothing like a Rivers Cuomo song to help you simplify and remember that less is more.

When we left the boat, this song was almost finished. Here's our co-creation.

> We wondered aloud what compelled us to travel this country playing the songs we wrote to small groups of people.

Rise

I'm a road junkie following worn tracks
Across the Great Plains where buffalo roamed way back
I hear the Ghost Dancers' song on the wind
Telling me there's no answer
Only wilderness within

I want to go there
I want to go there
I want to rise

To the steps of the mountain lion outrunning your machine
You can bring your chainsaw, but you can't cut what you can't see
Dragonflies hum out past the metal and steel
I sit by the water 'til the water reveals
That the lone wolf is no longer, I know the rhythm's getting fast
I know the middle of the river is the only way we can pass

Why don't we go there?
Why don't we go there?
Why don't we go there?
Why don't we rise?

You know that feeling when you know what's right
But you don't know why
Why don't we go there?

I'm going back to what I can't remember
I'm going back to what I can't remember
I'm going back to what I can't remember
I'm going back to what I can't remember

I want to go there
I want to go there
I want to go there
I want to rise

You know that feeling when you know what's right
But you don't know why
Why don't we go there?

Reflection Questions ···

What does this song mean to you?

Have you ever felt like you knew something to be true, but you didn't know how you knew it?

What is your connection to nature?

Have you ever felt like you could feel the "aliveness" of a place? Have you ever felt the energy of the things that happened there before?

Creativity Keys: Courage and Deep Listening

For this song to be born, I had to travel on a huge oceanliner (truth be told I hate cruises) and share my ideas and feelings with people I barely knew.

Also, it required kindness in the form of deep listening. Beth, Shannon and I listened deeply to and appreciated each other's experiences. As a result, nobody held back. If we hadn't felt safe, we might not have shared as much, and the song might not be as rich as it is.

to the light

One snowy winter morning in 2010, I walked a wooded trail in Western Massachusetts while drinking a cup of hot coffee. As my boots crossed the soft deep snow, I hummed a melody with the words, "I can live without you, just not without loving you, so I let you go, even though I'm still loving you." This became the chorus of "I Still Love You," a song that claims you can let go of people you still love.

For years after this song's arrival, I sang it, however I often felt guilty because I hadn't given the opposite and prior feeling its due. Letting go hurts and it can take a long time. Whether it's due to a calling, life circumstances or death, I wanted to honor that real human feeling. What do we often do before we let go of someone we love? We hold on like crazy.

This holding on reminded me of the Siddhartha Buddha story. In it, it's predicted that Siddhartha will grow up to be either a great king or a spiritual leader. Siddhartha's father hopes he'll become the former and so he shields him from the outside world, raising him in a lavish palace entertained by dancing women, educated by brahmin and trained in archery and swordmanship*. But one day, Siddhartha leaves the castle and sees a sick man, an old man and a corpse*. As he has not yet experienced suffering, he feels moved to discover its root and how to transcend it. That day, Siddhartha leaves his family and begins his spiritual journey.

> # How do those who are left behind feel?

In the verses of this song, this ancient story is paired with two modern ones: Siddhartha begins a quest, a woman responds to her future children, and a child is called to a short life here on earth and then is called back home again. Knowing we are graced with each encounter, no matter how brief, how can the child's family welcome her and then let her go?

*Fields, Rick. (1997). "Who Is The Buddha? The life story of the historical Buddha, Siddhartha Gautama". *Tricycle: The Buddhist Review*, Spring 1997. Retrieved from tricycle.org/magazine/who-was-buddha-2

To the Light

The king said to his son
You know you're royal blood
Though your mother always warned me you'd be leaving
Inside these castle walls I thought
You wouldn't hear the call
Still the prophet in your heart started speaking

But I won't let you go even if it's to the light
I won't let you go even if it's to the light
I won't let you go even if it's to the light
Even though I know

She heard the voices of children
Coming through her heart
Children that could be hers
If she would only start
But she loved a man who could not play
A father's part
She said I leave you my love
For the ones who call, and he said

I won't let you go even if it's to the light
I won't let you go even if it's to the light
I won't let you go even if it's to the light
Even though I know

The best I have I give you
And now you're going to fly
To take your place among the stars
And illuminate our night

Come back come back come back
I won't let you go
Come back come back come back
I won't let you go

Little baby Grace
She came down from above
The hole in her heart
Opened us to love
We didn't know we needed her
But she answered all our prayers
She could not stay away
Once her name was called

I won't let you go even if it's to the light
How do I let you go even if it's to the light?
I won't let you go even if it's to the light even though I know
Oh I won't let you go even if it's to the light
How do I let you go even if it's to the light?
I won't let you go even if it's to the light even though I know

The best I have I give you
And now you're going to fly
To take your place among the stars
And illuminate our night

Reflection Questions ··

What have you learned from letting go?

When is a time you had to let go of someone and could see it was for the best? When is a time you had to let go of someone and couldn't see it was for the best?

What does it mean to let someone go?

Can you love someone and let them go? If so, how?

Creativity Keys: Patience and Asking for Help

This song required patience and the willingness to ask for help. It changed at least twenty times over a four-year period. One day, when I knew I was close, I wondered: Who can help me finish this odd, intricate, layered song? Jennifer Kimball! So we jumped on Skype and she helped me tease out the final verse lyrics.

let yourself be

I was sitting at the piano in my parents' house. It was a few days after my 5-week old nephew Mikey had died. I wasn't writing a song, I was doing anything I could to make it through the agony and fear I felt after his passing. I played simple chords and sang "You can make it, you can make it," as if singing to my brother and sister-in-law. Would they survive their loss? If I kept repeating those words, could I make them true?

As I played, I was reminded of another recent loss of my college friend Cathy. She'd requested I play "Let it Be" at her funeral and I'd wrestled with how to let her death be.

"When I find myself in times of trouble, Mother Mary comes to me, speaking words of wisdom, let it be. In my hour of darkness, she is standing right in front of me, speaking words of wisdom, let it be."

I also recalled the difficult birth of my daughter Cecilia and how my doula had said at the height of the pain, "let yourself be." Immediately,

I thought of Cathy and the words to "Let It Be" and I understood my doula to mean that the only way to make it through is to allow yourself to go through the pain, to not fight it, to be as you are.

A year later, the melody to "you can make it" floated back into my awareness and I decided to add the words "let yourself be" after them.

But then, ironically, I didn't let the song be. I worried it was too sad so I turned it into something else and then abandoned it. Luckily, six years later, the original melody and words returned to me in a meditation and within days I recorded it. I'm grateful to share it with you now.

> I understood my doula to mean that the only way to make it through is to allow yourself to go through the pain, to not fight it, to be as you are.

Let Yourself Be

When we were kids you know
I thought you were the sun
Like flowers we'd turn to you
Your warmth for everyone

Now it's black every morning
It's black every night
You still rise

You can make it
You can make it
You can make it
Just let yourself be

You've got someone to love
Someone who loves you back
And we're all here for so few years anyway

Still it's black every morning
It's black every night
You still rise

You can make it
You can make it
You can make it
Just let yourself be

Reflection Questions ···

Recall a time you allowed what wanted to be, to be. How did you allow it? How did you not censor? What did it take for you to surrender?

Have you ever experienced a series of synchronicities that made you pay attention? What were they?

What is your experience with pain? Have you ever created more pain as a reaction to the initial pain?

Have you ever fully allowed pain? Did this help dissipate it or not?

Creativity Key: Surrender

Sometimes a song evolves over a long period of time and requires the intersection of multiple events in order to be born.

For this song to exist, I had to surrender. When the song eventually returned in its original form during meditation, I had to trust and respect that it knew what it wanted to be (almost like it was a person). The other key was paying close attention, witnessing and noticing clues. I had to be willing to integrate things from seemingly unrelated experiences; to have faith that there was a thread between them.

hymn of hope

This past year, my friend Mark suggested I read Anne LaMott's *Almost Everything: Notes on Hope*. He said it helped him when the news was bad. In recent years, I'd let hope fall into a category of less-than virtues. Having read inspirational writers who urged the reader to *intend instead of hope, do instead of hope*, or *decide instead of hope*, I'd inadvertently forgotten about including hope as part of the equation.

I began to rekindle my relationship with hope while reading her book. Hope, not for a specific outcome (although that's wonderful), but hope more in a general sense, a hope that allows for the possibility of something good emerging even if we don't know what it is yet.

Right around the same time, I was writing songs for oncology nurses as part of Songs for the Soul, a research project in which songwriters meet with oncology nurses and write songs for them based on their stories.

One of the nurses I met talked about how her work was so emotionally challenging that she spent her commute *deciding* to bring hope to her day, to her patients. Their prognosis was not good, but she decided she had to bring hope anyway. This really struck me. I told her I'd been led to believe there were more powerful options than hope, but that I was doubting this now. Maybe hope could include action, intention and decision.

> I began to rekindle my relationship with hope while reading Anne Lamott's book. Hope, not for a specific outcome (although that's wonderful), but hope more in a general sense, a hope that allows for the possibility of something good emerging even if we don't know what it is yet.

In writing a song for this nurse based on her individual story, this hymn also emerged. Through the alchemy of Anne Lamott's book, Mark's email and this particularly compassionate nurse, it popped out in about five minutes as I sat down at a friend's piano. It was as if the song already existed and was just waiting for someone to pull it through.

Hymn of Hope

I carry hope in my heart
Even when I don't feel hope
I decide, I decide
To make a home in my heart
Even as the darkness sets
I do my best
So I can rest
Knowing there is hope in my heart

I carry hope in my heart
The only way to heal the scars
This side of heaven
So I'll intend to make a home in my heart

I carry hope in my heart
Even when I don't feel hope
I decide, I decide
To make a home in my heart
Even as the darkness sets
I do my best
So I can rest
Knowing there is hope in my heart
In my heart
In my heart

Reflection Questions ···

What does hope mean to you?

When, if ever, have you actively cultivated hope in your life and how did it affect you/turn out?

Can hope by itself ever be a negative?

What does it mean to have hope?

Creativity Key: Beliefs

We create according to our beliefs. How cool is it when new information allows us to question our beliefs enough to let a new perspective emerge? Months earlier, I had no intention of writing a song about hope. Through my interactions with others however, I opened up enough to let this song come through.

the donut song

I was out of town and my husband, Frank, was in charge of our daughters. When I returned, Frank told me that our 5-year-old, who loves food and eats it with unadulterated pleasure, had asked to eat her donut in the car on the ride home from the donut shop. He told her she couldn't and explained they needed to keep the car clean. She could eat it once they got home.

"I just want to *hold* the donut, I'm not going to eat it yet," she said.

When Frank told me this, we laughed, both thinking the same thing: *Yeah, right*. Then Frank broke into a semi-Journey-the-band-esque voice singing, "*I just want to hold the donut, I'm not gonna eat it yet!*" over a spontaneous, made-up melody and we laughed even harder. An idea was born.

"We should write this 'Donut song'," one of us said. But as busy working parents, we thought, "But when?" Later that year, we had the rare opportunity to be sitting on a beach in Hawaii when Frank said, "Hey, let's write that song!"

> I just want to *hold* the donut, I'm not going to eat it yet.

It was so fun, that it occurred to us that maybe we should *only* write songs from kids' points of view and *only* write them on beaches.

The Donut Song

Is it our turn yet?

Why is there such a long line?

I want chocolate

Chocolate with sprinkles this time

Can I eat it now?

Ok, not in the car

I can eat it at home

But home is so far

I just wanna hold the donut

I'm not gonna eat it yet

I just wanna hold it

I'm not gonna eat it yet

Why are we stopping here?

Can I have one too?

He gets a toy for his birthday

But I never do

So can I eat it now?

Yes my seatbelt is on

I promise I won't spill

Oh come on

I just wanna hold the donut

I'm not gonna eat it yet

I just wanna hold it

I'm not gonna eat it yet

Mom, mom, mommy, mama, mom, dad?

I just wanna hold the donut

I'm not gonna eat it yet

I just wanna hold it

I'm not gonna eat it yet

Reflection Questions ··

Have you ever tried to get into the mindset of a child? What was that like?

When, if ever, has thinking or playing in a childlike way brought more joy into your life?

Have you ever created something spontaneously? If so, what was it?

Have you ever had a really silly idea that you let yourself follow through on? Why or why not?

Creativity Key: Alchemy

With this song, an experience we would've forgotten in a few days turned into something we'll always remember. Instead of having our creativity be separate from our day-to-day, The Creativity Key of Alchemy invites us to let them mix and inform each other. There's no separation between our experiences and our writing other than the separation we make by deciding what's worth writing about and what isn't. We started writing about this *purely* for the fun of it, and something emerged. With alchemy one thing is turned into another and anything can be used for fodder. What can you make alchemy out of this week?

acknowledgements

Thank you to Natalia Zukerman and Meg Hutchinson for your friendship, moral, and technical support. Thank you Greg "Stryke" Chin, Liam Davis, Mona Tavakoli and Alex Wong for helping me bring these songs to life. Thank you to all the musicians, songwriters and sound engineers who contributed in some way to these songs including Duke Levine, Mai Bloomfield, Chaska Potter, Steve Dawson, Beth Wood, Shannon McNally, Jennifer Kimball, Laura Donohue, Houda Zakeri, Javier Dunn, Erin Zindle, Lewis Rawlison, Geoff Michael, Tom Polce and Justin Hergett. Thank you Jen Lee for helping to identify the primary story in each of these stories. Thank you Barbara Heaton for your artistry. Thank you designer Liz Kalloch. An enormous thank you to my partner Frank Marotta, Jr. for your musical, technical, editorial and video support, and to my nuclear and extended family. To RCM and HPSM for song seeds and for singing and to all who appear in these pages. A deep thank you to my Kickstarter family who made this possible. May the love and kindness you share return to you over and over again.

The songs in this collection are available on the enclosed CD as well as through iTunes, Apple Music, Spotify and other streaming services.

Made in the
USA
Middletown, DE

77527263R00045